I Admit Nothing

John Yamrus

Epic Rites Press

I Admit Nothing © 2016 by John Yamrus. Exterior photograph copyright © 2016 by Tracy Lee Landers. All rights reserved. No part of this book may be used or reproduced in any manner whatsoever without written permission except in the case of brief quotations embedded in critical articles and reviews.

First edition. Printed in the USA.

Editor: Wolfgang Carstens
Exterior photograph: Tracy Lee Landers

Exterior: Richard Robert Hansen
www.poems-for-all.com

ISBN: 978-1-926860-53-4

Epic Rites Press publications are distributed worldwide by Tree Killer Ink. For more information about *I Admit Nothing* (and other books and publications from Epic Rites Press) please visit the Epic Rites website at www.epicrites.org, the Tree Killer Ink website at www.treekillerink.com, or address Tree Killer Ink / Epic Rites Press: 33 Sioux Road, PO Box 80002 Woodbridge, Sherwood Park, Alberta, Canada T8A 5T4, or contact Wolfgang Carstens at info@treekillerink.com.

Epic Rites: any press is only as "small" as its thinking.

For Kathy

Contents

when 9

we 10

he was afraid 11

there's 12

the cigarette 13

if 14

give me poetry 15

it 16

the only thing 20

A. Lotta Nevada 18

it's amazing 20

i pulled 22

miracles 23

"i get 24

find 25

they 26

and 27

the apartment 28

the streets 29

there is 30

if 31

a review 32

i remember 33

first 34

Jesus, ... 35

i've 36

there 37

i swear, ... 38

the 39

Mr. Connor 40

he 41

my 42

give me 43

he 44

hemingway 45

this chair 46

the writers... 47

the knees 50

Landon 54

the 55

if 50

"so," he said, ... 56

charley 58

my 59

the cashier 60

the hell with 61

she 62

he 63

his scribbled review 64

some guy, ... 65

even if 68

I Admit Nothing

John Yamrus

Epic Rites Press

when

i
sent
the magazine

a
poem
that was
one word long,

he
said
what the
hell is this?

i
said

art.

we

did a
midnight
Chinese run

and sat
in the kitchen

just
brother
and sister

eating
egg drop
and won-ton

and
neither

time

nor
distance

nor
years

meant
a single
god-damn thing.

he was afraid

to fail.

his poems
were

all
quite safe

and
measured.

just like

his
life.

i
felt
sorry
for the guy.

he'd
never know

how
it felt

to
stare
death in the eye

and
smile.

there's

a
picture
of him,

looking out a window.

short brimmed hat.

red tie.

they say
he was good at what he did.

i'll never know.

the cigarette

burned
low,

and
he leaned
over to smother it
on the table near the bed.

as he
pressed the stub

in
the tray,

he
heard

the
knock
on the door.

if

you
want
your poems

to
be
real,

live them,

don't
write them.

give me poetry

that's new.

that fails.

that makes mistakes.

give me poetry
that you don't know
what in the world you need to name it.

give me poetry
that bleeds from the eyes

and
shouts at the world.

give me poetry that stands naked and beaten,
with its back against the wall,
still screaming
i am now!

it

started
in high school,

with
the pictures
he left on the boys room sink.

in college,
there was Roberta,
but, she was a dick

and she
was a failure, too.

none of
the jobs worked out...

not
selling light bulbs door to door...

or,
magazines...

or,
that year
he spent in
his uncle's store,
delivering lampshades

and
couches
and rugs...

nothing
seemed to work.

it,
and him,
and she and her...

they all
failed him.

but,
the one thing
he could always count on...

the
one thing
he knew for sure...

is
when
it came right down to it,

there'd
always be

a
knot

at
the end
of his rope.

A. Lotta Nevada

was
the name
she went by.

she
wrote
bad poetry,

had
metal studs
in her lips and nose,

and
tattoos
on her neck, arms
and the finger she gave to everyone.

she
smoked, drank,
didn't give a shit...

and
was the
most beautiful thing
you ever saw in your life,

which
made it all
the more disconcerting

when
she got the knife.

George
never even
saw it coming.

they
buried him
in his brown suit,

with
a grey tie.

on the last day
they brought
the dog.

the only thing

dumber
than a writer,

is
someone
who admits
to being a writer.

i am
5 foot 7,

65
years old,

and i
love dogs.

i am
not dumb,

and
i admit

nothing.

it's amazing

how
quickly
you come to accept

and
even love

smudge marks
on the windows…

toys
everywhere…

even
the poop in the yard.

that
part's easy…

it's
when
they're gone…

that's
really hard.

i pulled

the
shades

in the
hotel room.

i turned off
the t.v.

i
kept
it dark.

it
was
6 hours

till
my reading.

this
was a part of me

they
could
never ever

have.

miracles

are
a dime
a dozen

and
salvation's

just
another
one of your

bad
ideas.

what
the hell
are you talking about?

she
said as
he laid his head

down
on the bar.

nothin'...

just
talking to a guy

who
used to be
a friend of mine.

"i get

my
brown
from coffee,

and
my black
from eights."

he
dropped
the mic and left.

the
poets
in the audience

didn't know
what the hell he meant.

the
waiter

smiled.

find

the
poem,

eat
the words,

and
carry on.

they

called
him

Ballrush.

don't
ask me,

and
don't ask him,

because
neither of us

know.

one
day,
Ballrush

got
a pistol,

a
rifle,

a
pocket
full of shells,

and
made those people
remember that name forever.

and

as
a very
respected
writer of poetry,

how
(ma i ask)

do
you get
your exercise?

opening
wine bottles.

the apartment

had
no heat,
no hot water
and no back door.

to
make it
interesting
two strippers
lived upstairs,

the problem was
they were nice girls.

broke,
just like us.

we ate
boiled noodles

and
very little else.

the
poems
came hard.

the streets

are
dark,

and
it's not

only
the night.

there is

nothing
better

than
the smell

of a
sleeping dog.

if

they're
telling you
your writing's good,

don't
believe them.

what
they're saying
is you're giving them
something they've seen before.

don't
be safe.

fall
on your face.

try
something new.

try
something new.

try.

a review

of my
latest book

laughed at
my having a poem

only
three words long.

in
response,

i
wrote
another,

one
word long.

it
was:

"endure."

i
figure

i'll wait
the bastards out.

i remember

the
porch

the
grey paint

the
swing

the
flowers

the
awning

and
the hedges.

my
god,

i
remember

the
hedges.

first

you
dream,

then

you
die

Jesus,

don't
tell me...

don't
offer....

don't
suggest...

don't
infer...

anything...

just

let
me

be.

i've

got a
bloody nose.

the
blood

is
bright,

red

and
urgent.

i
love

it.

there

was
a time

i
was
afraid

of
nothing.

i swear,

one of
these days

i'll
get it

right.

the

royalty
check came.

it
was nice
seeing money

for
something
i had written.

the
wine store
was 7 minutes away.

Mr. Connor

was
fat and old,

(he
was 45
at the time)

and he
swung a pick
with as much violence
as i've ever seen in my life.

he
wore
a baseball cap,

wiped
his face
with a rag,

and
blew his
nose with his finger.

it
was
1962.

two years later,
he was
dead.

he

sat
all day,
listening to
old Lennie Tristano records.

the dog's
bowl was empty.

outside,
the box was
filled with newspapers and mail.

he
hadn't
taken a bath in a week.

life
sure was good.

he
put on
another record,

filled
the dog's bowl,

and
sat back
on the couch.

my

poems
are not meant

to
impress you.

they
are written

to
help me

make it
thru the night.

give me

wine,
my wife,
and maybe

a
dog.

that's
all i need.

and
you can
shoot me now.

he

didn't
know what
he had to do next.

he
only
knew
he had to.

hemingway

had
the final word
about grace under pressure.

hemingway

was
an ass.

this chair

where i sit
and write my poems
is beat up and scratched,
held together with wire, tape and hope.

you figure it out.

the writers...

bore
me.

the
professors
who brag about
just having paid $1,000

to
take
a workshop

with
this one,

or
that.

then
they put it
on their resumes,

like
it matters:

"Karla
has taken
workshops with

him
and her

and
this and

that.

she
has also
rec'd a grant,

an
award
from here…

a
prize
from there…

and a
fellowship
from who knows where.

she's a
full professor

of
literature.

she's
published
an article on Pound.

and
lectured

on the
social relevance
of Thompson's *Seasons.*"

she's never
missed a car payment,

had a man
walk out on her,

or,
fell asleep
on the kitchen floor.

her
next class
starts at two.

if

you
can't
figure out
that my poems

have
no titles,

call
this one
ucanhaveyrfuckincityback

and put
d.a. levy's
name on it.

the knees

are
gone.

i no
longer drink.

my
days
of tequila
are a thing of the past.

more
often than not,
i'm in bed by nine.

steps
are a challenge.

i
have
some kid
who cuts the grass.

it's all
different now.

it
seemed
to happen over night.

i
guess
that's just

the way it goes.

change
(like they say),

is
inevitable.

but,
the one thing
that will never change...

for
now,
at least...

after
i climb
the stairs...

after i
take my pills,

prop
the pillows,

pull
the covers,

flip
the lights...

there
will still
be me and you,

and
that dog
between us,

with
her dirty feet

and
stinking breath...

and
the rest of the world

will
have to
wait its turn.

Landon

got
drunk
on a gallon
of MD 20/20,

and
spent
the night

on the kitchen floor,

looking
for Van Gogh's

other ear.

the

sad
thing…

the
wonderful

thing…

the
glorious

thing…

is

i
don't think
i'll ever be able

to
finish
this poem.

"so," he said,

"your book
is called Alchemy?

did you know
that in the middle ages

they believed
you could make gold

out of
everyday things?

of course,
it was

a
false

and
useless

science.

they
called that
Alchemy, too!"

i paid
for my wine,

took
my change

and left.

sometimes
the obvious

is all
the inspiration

you need.

charley

had
bad teeth

and
had never
been in love.

he
drank
red wine
in the morning,

and
hated
having to
go to work.

the gun
was convenient.

my

cries
of urgency,

fear

and
remorse,

are
heard

only
by ghosts.

the cashier

at the
pharmacy
tells me he's a writer.

trying
to be polite,

i ask
what he's working on.

"nothing.

i'm waiting
for the inspiration."

i
didn't
know how to answer that,

so,
i paid for my gum,

and
walked out…

inspired.

the hell with

poetry,
poets,
writers,

workshops
and books...

let me
tell you about
the 1961 Yankees.

she

knew
it.

and
he knew it.

that time
was far past

and
gone.

he

couldn't
tell if it was
blood or wine.

he
had no
cuts on him,

so,
he knew.

and that
didn't make it

any
better.

he
only knew
he needed more.

his scribbled review

meant
to read:

THAT'S
not poetry...

but,
in his haste

he
wrote:

WHAT'S
not poetry...

either way,

he
was
right.

some guy,

pissed at my
refusal

at this
late stage
in the game

to
call myself

a
poet,

wrote to me,
asking:

"so,
what is it, then?

just
words on a page?

is
that
all it is

to
you?"

i
guess
he wanted me
to say the words were deathless,

precious,

golden…

maybe
he figured
it would reflect

back
on him…

but,
i had
nothing.

i
didn't
know what to say,

and
i didn't
feel like making
him feel any better.

so,
i wrote back,

saying:

nah,
it's just
putting one foot
in front of the other.

i
never
heard from him again.

even if

the
poems
get ignored,

the
work
gets done,

and
your life

is
saved.

About John Yamrus

Since 1970 John Yamrus has published 25 volumes of poetry and 2 novels. He has also had more than 1,800 poems published in print magazines around the world. Selections of his poetry have been translated into several languages, including Spanish, Swedish, French, Japanese, Italian, Romanian, Albanian and most recently Bengali. His poetry is taught in several colleges and universities. His website is www.johnyamrus.com.

Also by John Yamrus

Burn
Endure
Alchemy
Bark
They Never Told Me This Would Happen
Can't Stop Now!
Doing Cartwheels On Doomsday Afternoon
New And Selected Poems
Blue Collar
Shoot The Moon
One Step at a Time
78 RPM
Keep The Change
New And Used
Start To Finish
Someone Else's Dreams (novel)
Something
Poems
Those
Coming Home
American Night
15 Poems
Heartsongs
Lovely Youth (novel)
I Love

CPSIA information can be obtained
at www.ICGtesting.com
Printed in the USA
BVHW09s0832090718
521160BV00032B/1857/P